SCIENCE ACTIVITIES

LIGHT
— AND —
COLOR

VOLUME 6

Tom Jackson

GROLIER
EDUCATIONAL

Published 2002 by Grolier Educational
Sherman Turnpike,
Danbury, Connecticut 06816

FOR BROWN PARTWORKS

Project editor:	Lisa Magloff
Deputy editor:	Jane Scarsbrook
Text editors:	Caroline Beattie, Ben Morgan
Designer:	Joan Curtis
Picture researcher:	Liz Clachan
Illustrations:	Mark Walker
Index:	Kay Ollerenshaw
Design manager:	Lynne Ross
Production manager:	Matt Weyland
Editorial director:	Anne O'Daly
Managing editor:	Bridget Giles
Consultant:	Donald R. Franceschetti, PhD University of Memphis

Printed and bound in Hong Kong

Set ISBN 0-7172-5608-1
Volume ISBN 0-7172-5614-6

Library of Congress Cataloging-in-Publication Data
Science Activities / Grolier Educational
    p. cm.
    Includes index.
    Contents: v.1. Electricity and magnetism—v.2. Everyday Chemistry—v.3. Force and
motion—v.4. Heat and energy—v.5. Inside matter—v.6. Light and color—v.7. Our
Environment—v.8. Sound and hearing—v.9. Using materials—v.10. Weather and climate.
ISBN 0-7172-5608-1 (set : alk.paper)—ISBN 0-7172-5609-X (v.1 : alk. paper)—
ISBN 0-7172-5610-3 (v.2 : alk. paper)—ISBN 0-7172-5611-1 (v.3 : alk. paper)—ISBN
0-7172-5612-X (v.4 : alk. paper)—ISBN 0-7172-5613-8 (v.5 : alk. paper)—ISBN
0-7172-5614- 6 (v.6 : alk. paper)—ISBN 0-7172-5615-4 (v.7 : alk. paper)—ISBN
0-7172-5616-2 (v.8 : alk. paper)—ISBN 0-7172-5617-0 (v.9 : alk. paper)—ISBN
0-7172-5618-9 (v.10 : alk. paper)
    1. Science—Study and teaching—Activity programs—Juvenile literature. [1.
Science—Experiments. 2. Experiments] I. Grolier Educational (Firm)

LB1585.S335 2002
507.1'2—dc21

                                                    2001040519

ABOUT THIS SET

Science Activities gives children a chance to explore fascinating topics from the world of science using the same methods that professional scientists use to solve problems. This set introduces young scientists to the scientific method by focusing on the importance of planning experiments, conducting them in a rigorous fashion so that a fair test can be carried out, recording all the stages, and organizing and analyzing the data to draw conclusions. Readers will have the chance to conduct exciting and innovative hands-on activities and to learn how to record and analyze their experiments and results in a variety of ways.

Every volume of *Science Activities* contains 10 step-by-step experiments, along with follow-up activities that encourage readers to find out more about the subject. The activities are explained and enhanced with detailed introductory and analysis sections. Colorful photos illustrate each activity, and every book is packed full of pictures and illustrations explaining the details of each topic.

By working fun and educational experiments into the context of the scientific method, anyone using this set can get a feel for how professional scientists go about their work. Most importantly, just have fun!

PICTURE CREDITS
(b=bottom; t=top; l=left)

Art Explosion: 43, 56; **Corbis:** Betteman Archive 4, Cydney Conger 17, Dimitri Lundt 22, Bill Ross 5, Tim Thompson 51(b), Roger Antrobus 23, Michael Boys 51 (t), Danny Lehman 61; **Corbis/Digital:** World Panoramas 6; **European Southern Observatory (ESO):** 49; **F. Permadi:** 50; **Hulton Archive:** Joseph Niepce 38; **Image Bank:** Steve Allen 33, Grant V. Faint 12, 32, Joanna McCarthy 39, Henry Sims 11, Jody Dole 23, Rita Maas 37; **NASA:** 4 (t), 29, 56 (l), 61 (b); **Papillo:** Robert Pickett 16; **Science Photo Library:** Bill Reber/Eve Ritscher Associates 44, Dr. Jeremy Burgess front cover, 13, Geoff Thompkinson 45, Frank Zullo 28, Antonia Reeve 37; **Travel Ink:** Nick Battersby 27, Trevor Creighton 21.

CONTENTS

VOLUME 6
LIGHT AND COLOR

INTRODUCTION

Our planet is continually flooded by energy pouring out of the Sun. We see a lot of this energy as light, but the Sun produces invisible rays as well. Light and other types of rays are called electromagnetic radiation.

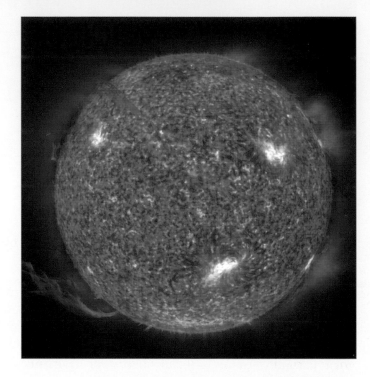

Light from the Sun takes about eight minutes to reach Earth. The Sun also sometimes produces huge explosions of gas, like the arc in the bottom left above.

There are many types of electromagnetic radiation, including x-rays, radio waves, heat, infrared light, ultraviolet light, and gamma rays. They are all very similar to light, but they vary in how much energy they contain.

Visible light is the range of electromagnetic radiation we can see. Cells in our eyes contain minute particles that are sensitive to light, and these particles convert light into electric pulses. Our brains then use the pulses to create pictures of the world.

Nearly all light energy comes from the Sun or other stars in the Universe. When a lightbulb glows, it uses electricity generated from fuel, such as coal, gas, or oil. These fuels formed over millions of years from trees and plants, which originally used the energy in sunlight to grow.

WAVE OR PARTICLE?

Until fairly recently, scientists were baffled by light. Some thought light was a stream of tiny particles, while others thought it moved as a wave, like ripples in a pond. We now know that both ideas are true.

Many famous scientists have studied light. In the 17th century the Dutch astronomer Christiaan Huygens (1629–1695) put forward the idea that light is a wave. But the

English scientist Isaac Newton (1642–1727) disagreed. He thought light had to be a stream of particles, because the edges of shadows are very sharp. Waves do not usually produce sharp-edged patterns. Water waves, for example, wash around objects, and sound waves can travel around corners.

The German-born U.S. physicist Albert Einstein (1879–1955) was the first to realize that the wave theory and particle theory were both correct. Einstein suggested that we think of light as tiny packets of energy, which we now call photons. Each photon has the characteristics of a wave. When viewed under a microscope, the "sharp"

The scientist Isaac Newton discovered that white light is really a mixture of all the different colors.

Life on Earth could not exist without sunlight. Plants capture the energy in sunlight, and use it to combine air molecules and water to make food.

edge of a shadow that confused Isaac Newton is not so sharp—light can be seen leaking around the edges of an object, as with other types of waves.

Einstein once asked himself a very important question: What would you see if you were traveling along on a beam of light? The answers he came up with turned into his special theory of relativity (1905), in which he stated that light always travels at exactly the same speed through empty space.

OPTICAL LAWS

Most of this book concerns a branch of science called optics. In optics we think of light as waves rather than particles. Waves of light behave like any other waves, such as water waves, air waves, or the seismic waves that travel through the ground during an earthquake. Every wave has a wavelength (the distance between the peak of one wave and the next) and a frequency (the number of times the wave travels a wavelength every second). Waves also have an amplitude, which is the height of the wave's peak or the depth of the trough.

Light acts in many surprising ways, as you will find out. It bounces off objects (reflects), bends as it passes through substances (refracts), ripples outward as it moves through slits (diffracts), spreads in all directions as it hits tiny particles (scatters), and interferes with itself, causing unusual patterns. However light behaves, it is always amazing.

The good science guide

Science is not only a collection of facts—it is the process that scientists use to gather information. Follow this good science guide to get the most out of each experiment.

• Carry out each experiment more than once. That prevents accidental mistakes skewing the results. The more times you carry out an experiment, the easier it will be to see if your results are accurate.

• Decide how you will write down your results. You can use a variety of different methods, such as descriptions, diagrams, tables, charts, and graphs. Choose the methods that will make your results easy to read and understand.

• Be sure to write your results down as you are doing the experiment. If one of the results seems very different from the others, it could be because of a problem with the experiment that you should fix immediately.

• Drawing a graph of your results can be very useful because it helps fill in the gaps in your experiment. Imagine, for example, that you plot time along the bottom of the graph and temperature up the side. If you measure the temperature ten times, you can put the results on the graph as dots. Use a ruler to draw a straight line through all the dots. You can now estimate what happened in between each dot, or measurement, by picking any point along the line and reading the time and temperature for that point from the sides of the graph.

• Learn from your mistakes. Some of the most exciting findings in science came from an unexpected result. If your results do not tally with your predictions, try to find out why.

• You should always be careful when carrying out or preparing any experiment, whether it is dangerous or not. Make sure you know the safety rules before you start working.

• Never begin an experiment until you have talked to an adult about what you are going to do.

ACTIVITY 1
REFLECTION

If you stand by a lake on a calm, sunny day, you might see a reflection on the surface of the water. Reflections happen because light rays bounce off objects as they hit them.

All objects reflect light. Smooth, shiny surfaces like mirrors and lakes produce the best reflections. They make light rays bounce away in one direction only, which is why they produce an image. Other objects make light rays bounce off in all directions, which makes their surface look dull and does not produce an image. If nothing reflected light, the whole world would be pitch black, except

Lakes produce reflections that turn everything upside down. If you stare straight down into a still lake, you can sometimes see clouds miles above.

for things that generate their own light, like the Sun, stars, and electric lights.

Light from the Sun or from lightbulbs looks white when we look at it directly, but it is really a

Reflecting color

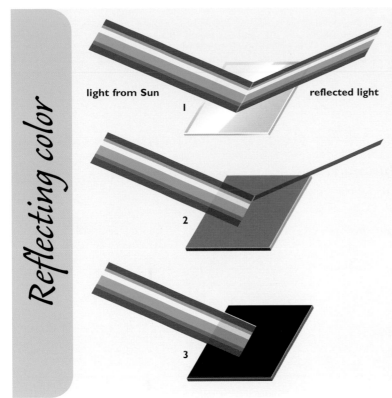

light from Sun   **reflected light**

1

2

3

Objects look colored because of the way they reflect light. White light, such as sunlight, is a mixture of light rays of all the different colors. White objects reflect all the colors together and therefore appear bright and white (1). Red objects absorb most colors but reflect the red light rays, and that is why they appear darker but red (2). Black objects absorb all the colors and reflect very little light, which is why they look so dark (3).

Light exists in different colors because it travels in waves. When the waves are far apart, the light has a long wavelength, and our eyes detect it as red. When the waves are closer together, our eyes see violet. The other colors have wavelengths between those of red and violet. Rays from the Sun that have wavelengths too long or too short for our eyes to detect are invisible to humans, but many other animals can see them.

mixture of all the different colors. When white light hits an object, the different colors are reflected in different amounts. Some colors are absorbed by the object, while others are reflected instead of being absorbed. The reflected colors are the ones we see. Limes look green, for instance, because they reflect green light but absorb other colors.

If an object reflects very little light, it has a black or very dark color. Instead of being reflected, most of the light is absorbed. A surface that reflects all the light that hits it looks white or shiny and mirrorlike. Reflection from mirrorlike surfaces is called specular reflection. Light reflected from other surfaces is called diffuse.

MIRROR IMAGES

An image in a mirror is different from the object producing it in one very important way: It is flipped from left to right. In other words, its left side appears on the right, and its right side appears on the left. For example, if you wink at yourself in a mirror with your left eye, you will see your right eye wink in the reflection. But up is still up, and down is still down.

Mirror images can be confusing. Try holding this page up to a mirror to see if you can read the reflection. All the words will be the wrong way around, but you might just be able to read it. An even harder task is to try writing in a mirror. Place a mirror in front of a piece of paper, and try to write your name so that you can read it normally in the mirror. You will have to write upside down and back to front at the same time!

USING MIRRORS

Before mirrors were invented, people had to look in pools of water or at pieces of polished metal to see themselves. Today we use mirrors for all sorts of jobs, not just to check how good we look.

Mirrors are essential in cars and trucks so that the driver can see what's on the road behind them. Another very important use of mirrors is in the telescopes that astronomers use to look at distant objects in space. The Hubble Space Telescope uses the world's largest and smoothest mirror to collect light from the faintest stars. Telescope mirrors are shaped like huge bowls to collect light over a wide area and focus it onto a small detector.

Two-way Mirror

ACTIVITY

Goals

1. Make a two-way mirror.
2. Combine your face with another person's face.

What you will need:

- piece of glass about 1 foot (30cm) square
- sheet of Mylar big enough to cover the glass. You can buy it from hardware stores as antiglare window film.
- cloth tape
- 2 electric lamps
- large blobs of modeling clay
- assistant

1 Cover one side of the glass with the Mylar film. Make sure the film lies flat against the glass.

2 Carefully tape the film to the edge of the glass with the cloth tape. Use more tape to cover the sharp edges of the glass.

Suspect behavior

Mirrors similar to the one you have made here are used in police stations when victims of crime are asked to identify a criminal. A suspect, along with a selection of members of the public, stands in a brightly lighted room looking at themselves in a mirror. On the other side, in a much darker room, the victim and police officers can look through the mirror without being seen by the people in the lineup. The police must be careful not to turn on the lights in their room in case the suspect sees who is giving evidence against him or her.

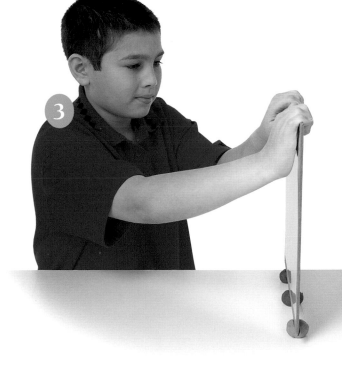

3 Set the mirror in the blobs of modeling clay so that it stands upright on a table. If you don't have modeling clay, use stacks of heavy books held together with rubber bands. Make sure the mirror is steady before you let go.

4 Place the lamps on the table, then make the room as dark as possible by closing the drapes and turning out all the lights. Sit on either side of the mirror so that you are facing each other. Take turns switching on the lamps to illuminate your faces while you look at the mirror. Try this with one light at a time, then try with both lights on together.

FOLLOW-UP   Two-way mirror

With a bit of practice you can use the two-way mirror to combine your faces together to make a strange, ghostly apparition. The easiest way to do that is to use lamps with dimmer switches. If you don't have dimmer lamps or a dimmer attachment, use flashlights instead.

Repeat the activity, but this time keep both lamps switched on. Look into the mirror so that you are facing each other directly. One of you should then slowly make their lamp dimmer (or slowly move the flashlight beam away from their face). The person on the dark side will gradually see their reflection fade and the image of the other

person grow stronger. Adjust your position so that your eyes, nose, and mouth are lined up as closely as possible. If you keep adjusting the brightness of the lamps, you should be able to blend the two faces together. When the faces merge, try opening your mouths together or blinking at the same time to see what it looks like.

ANALYSIS
Reflection

The mirror you made is not very different from others in your house. However, unlike those mirrors, it is two-way. That means some light reflects off each side, while some travels through the mirror to the other side.

The mirror in your bathroom reflects all the light that hits it. It is probably made of glass with a thin layer of silver or aluminum paint behind it. Behind that is a layer of wood or the wall. Light only comes from one side—the side you look at—so you can only see objects on that side of the mirror.

A two-way mirror can form images from both sides. That is because there is no wall or wood behind it, so both sides reflect light.

Unlike a bathroom mirror, which reflects all the light hitting it, clean window glass lets nearly all the light hitting it pass through. In other words, it transmits light. A two-way mirror also transmits light, but not all of it. About half the light hitting it is reflected back to the observer, while the other half passes through to the person on the other side.

LOOK ON THE BRIGHT SIDE

In the main activity you should have been able to see a reflection of your face when your lamp was switched on. When your partner's light was off, very little light would have passed through from the other side, so nearly all the light you saw in the mirror was reflected from your side. As a result, the only thing you could see was your reflection.

When your light was off and your partner's light was on, you should have seen something very different. Because your side of the mirror was dark, very little light was being reflected, but much more was coming through from the other side. You should have seen your partner's face in the mirror, perhaps with a faint reflection of your own.

DIM AND DIMMER

When both lights were on, you probably saw only your own reflection, but you might also have seen a very faint image of the other person. If you had dimmer lights and made both lights dim, the image of the other person would have grown a little stronger.

In the follow-up activity, as one lamp gets dimmer, the light coming through from the bright side becomes visible on the dark side. If the difference in brightness is great enough, only the view of the brighter side will be visible, though a ghostly reflection of the dim side might remain. On the bright side only the observer's reflection can be seen.

If you experimented for long enough with the dimmers or flashlights, you should have been able to make your faces merge together. Your brain, which is very good at recognizing the shape of a face, takes the images of both faces and joins them into one—even when the two sets of features are constantly changing.

Mirror mirror on the wall...

The angle at which a light beam hits a mirror is closely related to the angle of the reflected beam. A beam traveling at 90 degrees (right angles) to the mirror will be reflected straight back. That is because the angle of incidence (the angle of the incoming beam) is always the same as the angle of reflection (the angle of the reflected beam). The angle of incidence is measured from an imaginary line that is at 90 degrees to the mirror. Physicists call this line the "normal." A beam traveling at 20 degrees to the normal will create a reflected beam 20 degrees from the other side of the normal. That is why mirror images are back to front. The reflected light is identical to the incoming light, except that it is on the other side of the normal.

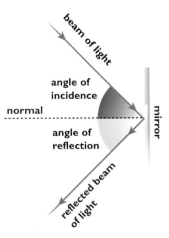

🔹 *Fairground mirrors produce a distorted reflection because the angle of incidence varies across the mirror's curved surface.*

ACTIVITY 2
INTERFERENCE

Just like water, light travels in waves that can combine and interfere with each other. Interference of light waves produces the shimmering colors on the surface of soap bubbles, on oily puddles, and on hummingbird wings.

Scientists think of light as a series of waves rolling through space. Light waves behave just like the ripples on a pond when a pebble is thrown in. The pebble causes waves to move out in a circle from the point where the pebble hits the surface. The light created in the Sun moves away in a similar way.

Compare the surf hitting a beach in Hawaii to the ripples you make in the bath. Both are waves, but the ocean waves are far bigger than the ones in the bath. We can measure a wave in several different ways. The height of a wave's crest is called the amplitude; an ocean wave has a much larger amplitude than a bath wave. The distance between the crest of a wave and the crest of the wave in front is the wavelength. And the number of wavelengths that a wave travels in a second is called the frequency.

When water waves collide, they combine to form complex interference patterns. Light waves behave in a very similar way.

Light waves have a frequency, amplitude, and wavelength, just as all waves do. Compared to water waves, though, their wavelengths are tiny, and their frequencies are very high. This makes light waves much harder to study.

Imagine two tanks of water. A weight is dropped from a certain height into one tank, and ripples with a frequency of one wavelength per second are produced. Half a second later an identical weight is dropped from the same height into the other tank. Identical ripples are produced, but the crests of the second set of waves are half a second and half a wavelength behind the first set. In fact, the first wave would be at a crest (+1 amplitude) when the second was in a trough (−1 amplitude). Imagine joining these two sets of waves together. The end result would be no waves at all. Waves such as these, that do not rise and fall at the same time, that do not match crest for crest and trough for trough, are described as being out of phase.

INTERFERING WAVES

Imagine doing the the same experiment with a single large tank of water. The weights would be dropped in different parts of the tank, and the waves would travel toward each other. What would you see when the waves met? The answer to that would depend on the phase of the waves.

When waves hit each other and combine, physicists say the waves are interfering with each other. Waves can interfere in two ways: Either they combine to make a bigger wave, or they cancel each other out to make a smaller wave or no wave at all. Waves that are in phase, that is, waves that reach their crests and troughs at the same time, make bigger waves. Waves that are out of phase cancel each other out.

When ocean waves interfere with each other, they produce rough, choppy water; but what about light waves? You can see what happens when light

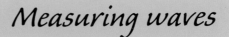

Measuring waves

Every type of wave has a wavelength (the distance between two crests) and an amplitude (the height of a crest or the depth of a trough). The wavelength of light is the property that determines its color.

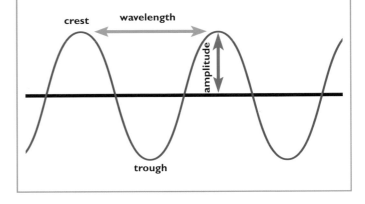

waves interfere by looking at soap bubbles. When light hits a soap bubble, it can do one of three things: It can pass through the film of water that makes up the bubble's skin; it can reflect off the top of the film; or it can reflect off the bottom of the film. The reflected light, therefore, comes from two slightly different places. As a result, the two sets of light waves are out of phase and interfere with each other. Some colors (wavelengths) of light cancel each other out, while others are strengthened and form a colorful pattern that changes if we alter our point of view.

Examples of interfering light waves are all around us. Cracked glass, coated eyeglass lenses, and oily puddles all produce shimmering colors thanks to interference. The iridescent colors of many animals form in the same way. The feathers of peacocks and hummingbirds, for example, produce color by interference, as do the scales of many butterflies and tropical beetles.

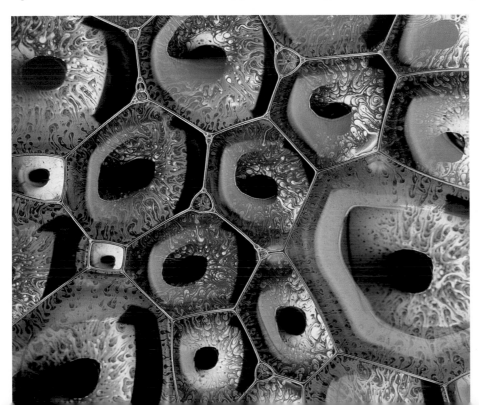

The beautiful colors on these soap bubbles are caused by light waves interfering with each other.

Make a Rainbow

Goals

1. **Create rainbow patterns of light interference.**
2. **Show that we see different wavelengths of light as different colors.**

What you will need:

- *2 squares of Plexiglas about 1 foot (30cm) square and about ⅛ inch (3mm) thick*
- *clean cloth*
- *soap and water*
- *tape and scissors*
- *piece of dark paper*
- *desk lamp*

1 Clean both sides of each Plexiglas square carefully with soap and water. Rinse with more water, then dry the surfaces with a soft, clean cloth.

2 Press both the squares of Plexiglas tightly together. Holding them in place, tape the edges together. You may need an assistant to help you do this.

3 Tape the black paper to one side of the Plexiglas "sandwich."

Troubleshooting

What if I can't see any rainbow patterns?

If you can't see colored patterns in the Plexiglas, separate the two sheets, and put a thin layer of engine oil on one of them. Ask an adult to help you do this. Then tape the sheets back together with the engine oil in the middle.

4 Hold the Plexiglas sandwich, papered side down, under a bright desk lamp.

5 You should see rainbow patterns in the Plexiglas, caused by the light waves interfering with each other. Carefully bend the Plexiglas sandwich, and watch how the patterns change.

FOLLOW-UP Make a rainbow

Another way to create colorful interference patterns is to make an oil slick. Put a few drops of engine oil or bicycle oil on a plate of water, and place your oil slick in sunlight. Oil floats on water, so after a few seconds it will spread to form a very thin film. Light rays reflected from the top and the bottom of the film will interfere and make colored patterns.

You can also make rainbow patterns with a CD. Use the back of the CD as a mirror to

reflect sunlight or a flashlight onto a piece of white paper, and a stunning rainbow will appear. The colors form because light reflects from tiny pits in a layer of aluminum in the CD. Light reflected from the bottom of the pits interferes with the rest of the reflected light, canceling out or boosting different colors.

Oily puddles make rainbow patterns because light reflected from the top and bottom of the oil film interferes.

ANALYSIS

Interference

The colored pattern you saw in the plastic was caused by interference. The white light from the lamp reflected off the bottom of the first sheet of Plexiglas, as well as off the top of the second sheet. The two sheets were separated by a very thin layer of air (or maybe oil). Because of this gap the two sets of reflected light waves were out of phase with each other. Colors appeared where they interfered—the equivalent of rough water on a lake.

White light is made up of many colors of light. The color of light is a measure of the light beam's wavelength. Our eyes detect the wavelength of the light, and our brain allots a standard color to it, which we then see. Red light has a longer wavelength than green light, for instance, and green light has a longer wavelength than blue light.

The pattern in the plastic was caused by certain wavelengths, or colors, in the white light being canceled out by destructive interference, leaving the other wavelengths of light to travel to your eye and be seen. The width of the gap between the plastic sheets affects which colors cancel each other out. If the gap is half the width of the wavelength of blue light, the two sets of waves will be sufficiently out of phase to cancel each other out completely. In reality the gap is many times wider than the wavelength of light, but it still affects the phases of both sets of waves in the same way. The gap between the two sheets is not perfectly level, so you should have seen different colors in different places. If you bent the plastic or squashed it, you would have seen the colored patterns spreading and changing as the width of the gap varied.

MAGNIFICATION

ACTIVITY 3

Have you ever wondered why magnifying glasses make everything look larger than life? In this chapter you can find out how to make a giant magnifying glass out of a goldfish bowl and use it to bend and focus light rays.

Light can travel through many substances, or media, such as water, glass, air, or a vacuum (a place with no matter). The speed of light is different for each medium. Light moves fastest through a vacuum and slows down as it enters another medium, like air. A change in light's speed causes a change in its direction as well.

AROUND THE BEND

Light bending in this way is called refraction. It occurs when a beam of light hits the boundary between two media at an angle. Scientists call the front of a light beam a wave front. A wave front could be thought of as an automobile axle with a wheel at either end. Imagine a wave front rolling through air toward a pane of glass. If the light beam is at an angle to the glass, one corner of the wave front—for example, the left—will hit the glass before the other. This will make the left side of the wave front change speed before the right.

Light bends when it passes between air and glass or water. The curved shape of a goldfish bowl bends the light even more, making objects look bigger.

Continuing the wheel-and-axle analogy, the wheel on the left slows down, while the one on the right goes on at the same speed—the axle begins to wheel around to the left. When the right corner of the wave front arrives at the glass, it too changes to the speed of the rest of the light beam, but by now the wave front is traveling in a different direction—the light has been refracted, or bent.

Lenses are transparent objects with a rounded surface. Because of their shape they bend light by refraction to a single point. We use lenses to "focus" light into an image that is a different size from the original. This is how telescopes make it possible to see objects that are very far away. Likewise, the lenses in microscopes magnify our view of things that are too small to see with the naked eye. Lenses work because they curve in opposite directions on each side. So, light bends one way as it enters a lens, then the opposite way as it leaves the lens.

Fishbowl Lens

Goals

1. **Create an image using a water lens.**
2. **Investigate how lenses work.**

What you will need:

- *round glass container*
- *water*
- *candle*
- *adult to light candle*
- *dish*
- *piece of thick white cardboard*
- *ruler*
- *newspaper (for follow-up)*

1 Fill the bowl with water. The water-filled bowl will be your lens.

Safety tip

Make sure an adult is with you throughout this activity. Keep the cardboard well away from the candle flame.

Lacemaker's lens

In the 18th century water lenses just like the fishbowl lens were used to focus light and to magnify fine details. Lacemakers used water lenses to help them see as they sewed delicate patterns in clothes. Glass lenses were also used to light fires by focusing light and heat from the Sun onto wood. Fires were sometimes started accidentally in this way.

2 Put the candle on a dish, and place it about 1 foot (30cm) from the lens. Ask an adult to light the candle.

Fuzzy image

The image formed by your fishbowl lens will probably be fuzzy and might consist of overlapping colors. The fuzziness is caused by different amounts of refraction happening in different parts of the bowl. The separate colors occur because some colors of light are refracted more than others.

3 Hold the cardboard against the lens on the opposite side from the candle.

4 Gradually move the cardboard away from the bowl. Stop when you see an image of the candle flame on the cardboard. How does this image compare to the flame itself?

Troubleshooting

What if I can't see an image on the board?

If your room is too bright, the light might drown out the candle's image. Try closing the drapes and turning out the lights to make the room darker. If the candle flame won't stop flickering, replace the candle with a small flashlight. Point the flashlight toward the bowl or, if possible, unscrew the top to expose the flashlight's bulb.

FOLLOW-UP — Fishbowl lens

Once you've made an image appear, prop the cardboard up with some books to keep it still. Then try moving the candle up and down, while keeping it the same distance from the lens. What happens to the image?

Now move the candle farther from the lens. What happens to the image on the cardboard? Put the candle down, and try to find the image by moving the cardboard.

Put the cardboard back with the books and the candle back in its original place. Now move the candle toward the lens. At what point can you no longer find an image on the cardboard?

Finally, place a newspaper behind the lens, and try reading the print. Do the words look bigger?

ANALYSIS — Magnification

The bowl of water works as a lens, focusing light from the candle onto the cardboard. The focused image is upside down; and when you moved the candle up and down, the image moved in the opposite direction. If you moved the candle away from the bowl, the image would have become blurred. If you then moved the cardboard toward the bowl, the image would have become sharp again. Likewise, if you moved the candle toward the bowl, you would have had to move the cardboard farther away to form an image. However, if the candle got too close to the bowl, it would have become impossible to form a sharp image again.

Light from the candle bends as it passes through the bowl. This is an example of refraction. As the light passes from air into glass, it slows down slightly, making the light turn if it hits the glass at an angle. It turns again as it enters the water, then passes through the center of the bowl and out into the air again. Refraction also occurs on the way out of the bowl, but this time the light bends in the opposite direction because of the bowl's spherical shape.

Because light travels in straight lines, light rays from any object normally spread out as they travel through the air. The fishbowl lens makes the spreading rays start traveling back toward each other. The point where they meet is called the focus, and that is where an image forms. The image is upside down because the light rays are flipped from top to bottom or left to right as they bend on their way through the lens.

All lenses have something called a focal length. It is the distance from the lens that light from a far object, such as a star, focuses to form an image. You can work out the focal length of your lens by using it to focus light from a bright light source more than 30 feet (9m) away, such as a streetlight or a full Moon. Using the cardboard in the same way as in the main activity, make an image of the object. (Don't use the Sun as your light source—you might set the

Microscopes use lenses to magnify things thousands of times. They allow scientists to study microorganisms and other things that are invisible to the naked eye.

paper on fire.) The distance from the center of the bowl to the image is the focal length of the lens. You can also use this technique to measure the focal length of a magnifying glass.

MAGNIFICATION

We can use lenses to make an object look bigger, or magnified. In the follow-up activity, the newspaper print appeared bigger through the fishbowl lens because it was less than one focal length away from the lens' center. Light sources closer than the focal length are too close to the lens for the light to be focused into an image on the other side. However, your eyes can complete the bending required to make a sharp image. The light that enters your eyes has already been bent by the lens, so when your brain turns the light into an image, the object looks bigger than it really is.

When several lenses are used together, they can magnify an image considerably. Microscopes use lenses in this way to make the tiniest objects big enough to see up close. Telescopes collect light from stars and planets millions of miles away and use multiple lenses to magnify the images.

Concave and convex

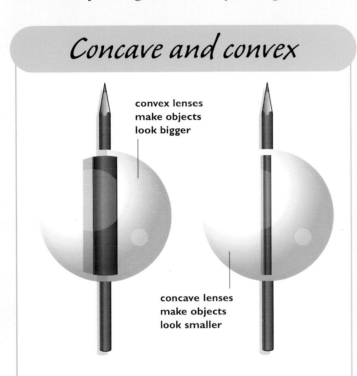

convex lenses make objects look bigger

concave lenses make objects look smaller

The focal length of a lens depends on its curve and what it is made of. Spherical lenses have shorter focal lengths than flatter lenses. Concave lenses, which are thinner in the middle than at the edges, have a negative focal length. That is because instead of focusing light, these lenses spread it out. As a result, concave lenses make objects look smaller instead of magnifying them. Eyeglass lenses are usually either concave or convex (rounded). They help correct the lens in the human eye, which sometimes doesn't make perfectly sharp images.

ACTIVITY 4
REFRACTION

Place a straw in a glass of water, and it will seem to bend where it enters the water. That happens because light from the straw changes direction as it moves out of the water. We call that refraction.

Nothing travels faster than light. However, the speed of light is not constant—it can change depending on what the light is passing through. Light moves fastest in space, slightly slower in air, slower still in water, and slowest in transparent (see-through) solids, such as glass.

When light moves from one substance, or medium, to another, its speed changes. It slows down when it passes from air to glass, for instance. If the light beam hits the new medium at an angle, the

Light bends when it moves from water into air. The ripples in a swimming pool bend the light in different directions, making objects under water look wobbly.

change in speed also makes the beam bend. This change in direction is called refraction.

To figure out how much a light beam refracts, we measure its angle. The angle is measured from the normal—an imaginary line at right angles to the surface of the glass, water, or other medium that the

Newton's prism

In 1666 the English scientist Isaac Newton (1642–1727) made an interesting discovery when he was studying a prism (a triangular wedge of glass). He found that a beam of sunlight passing through the prism bent and split into all the colors of the rainbow. That effect is caused by refraction. As light enters one side of the prism, it bends a little. Then it bends again as it leaves the prism. The different colors that make up white light bend by different amounts—violet the most, red the least, and other colors in between. Rainbows form in a similar way, but with billions of raindrops acting as separate prisms.

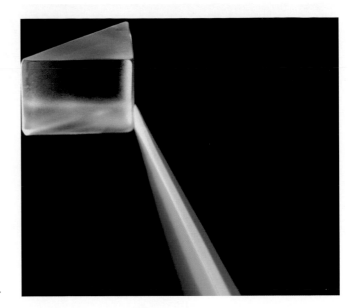

light is striking (see page 11). When light moves from a fast medium to a slower one, such as glass, it bends toward the normal. When it moves from a slow medium into a faster one, it bends away from the normal. If it moves between two mediums in which its speed is the same, it travels in a straight line.

Scientists compare the speed of light through any particular medium with the speed of light through space. This gives a number called the index of refraction. The slower the medium, the higher the index of refraction—and the more the light beam will bend as it enters the medium.

Light is slower in certain substances because the molecules (minute particles) in the substance slow its progress. There are no molecules in space, so light from the Sun travels at top speed all the way to Earth. We say space has a refractive index of one.

When light from the Sun enters our atmosphere, air molecules begin to slow it down. However, the molecules in air are spread out so thinly that the change in speed is tiny. Air has a refractive index very close to that of space—1.000293, to be precise. As a result, sunlight hardly bends at all when it enters the atmosphere.

Transparent (see-through) liquids, like water, are made up of molecules packed together more closely than in a gas. That slows the light significantly so a transparent liquid has a higher refractive index than a gas. See-through solids, like glass and diamond, are very tight collections of molecules. They slow down light even more than liquids. Diamond has the highest refractive index of all, at 2.419. Diamonds bend light so much it gets trapped inside and bounces around before escaping. That is the property that makes diamond sparkle.

Most solids aren't transparent. Instead of letting light pass through, they absorb or reflect the light, and that is why we can see them.

■ **Diamonds refract light so much they trap it inside and split the white light into twinkling colors.**

Disappearing Trick

Goals

1. **Investigate how different liquids slow down light.**

2. **Make a glass object disappear.**

What you will need:

- *2 glasses*
- *jug of water*
- *cooking oil*
- *baby oil*
- *2 glass stirrers or other small, clear glass objects*
- *corn syrup (to use in the follow-up activity)*

1 Place a glass in a bright place, but make sure there isn't a strong beam of light coming from just one direction. Pour water into the glass until it is one-third to one-half full.

2 Pour a thick layer of cooking oil on top of the water.

Fishy business

In some parts of the world fishers wade into the sea to catch fish one at a time with spears. Because of refraction, fish seen from above the water appear to be farther away than they really are, so the fishers compensate for this by aiming at a point that appears nearer than the fish.

Troubleshooting

What if the glass stirrers don't look faint in the oil?

The temperatures of the liquids affect the results in this activity. You might get better results on a cold day—when oil and water cool, they get denser, which makes them bend the light more. If the liquids are warm, put them in the fridge for an hour first.

Invisible animals

Many sea animals, such as jellyfish and plankton, have transparent bodies. Because their body tissue has almost the same refractive index as seawater, they are almost impossible to see, which helps them hide from predators.

3 Half-fill the second glass with baby oil.

4 Place the glass stirrers in the glasses, and look at the glasses from the side. What can you see? Are some parts of the stirrers fainter than others?

FOLLOW-UP Disappearing trick

The activity works even better if you use corn syrup instead of oil. Put a glass stirrer in a glass, and pour in corn syrup. The stirrer will vanish, but you might still be able to see a faint outline if you look closely.

Try the activity with different types of see-through materials. You could use marbles, Pyrex, old glasses, ice cubes, and plastic, for instance. Dunk a magnifying glass in oil or corn syrup, and see if it still magnifies things. To make Pyrex disappear, use a mixture of heavy and light mineral oils: two parts of heavy oil to one part of light oil.

ANALYSIS Refraction

In the main activity you should have noticed that the glass stirrer became faint or even disappeared where it passed through the cooking oil. It should have been easier to see in the baby oil and even easier to see in the layer of water below the cooking oil.

The stirrer disappears in liquids that have a refractive index similar to that of glass. Glass objects are transparent, which means we can see through them. But we can also see the glass itself. That is because some light reflects off the glass, allowing us to see details in the surface. Glass objects with a curved shape, such as the stirrers, also bend the light that passes through them, making whatever lies behind look distorted. That makes them even easier to see.

The glass stirrers bend light most when they are in air, because the refractive index of glass is very different from that of air. They bend light a bit less when they are in water, but they are still easy to see. Oil has a refractive index nearer that of glass, so light bends relatively little when it passes through the stirrers immersed in oil. That is why they appeared so faint. If you placed the stirrers in corn syrup, they would have become almost invisible. Corn syrup has the same refractive index as glass, so light passes straight through the stirrers without being distorted. A ghostly image of the stirrers probably remained, caused by slight imperfections in the glass.

USING REFRACTION

Police scientists use oils to calculate the refractive indexes of see-through materials found at crime scenes. They heat the oil until the material disappears. They know the refractive index of the oil at that temperature and so discover the refractive index of the sample. That helps them figure out where the material came from, which may provide vital clues.

Another way you can see the effects of refraction is to make a rainbow. Rainbows appear when sunlight shines on raindrops at a certain angle. The light bends (refracts) as it enters each raindrop, bounces (reflects) off the back of the drop, then bends again as it leaves. The different colors bend by different amounts and so separate, as in a prism.

Make a rainbow with a garden sprinkler or a mist-sprayer. Stand with the Sun behind you on a sunny morning or afternoon, and sprinkle water in front of you. How many colors can you count? Jump through the rainbow to see if you can still see it from the other side.

▶ *When sunlight passes through drops of water, the different colors reflect and refract in slightly different directions, producing a rainbow.*

Shimmering mirages

Mirages—the visions seen in deserts—are caused by refraction of light through hot air. When the ground gets very hot, the layer of air just above it heats up and expands, making its refractive index lower. Light from plants, rocks, or the sky is bent by this hot air and so appears to be coming from the ground. If the sky is clear, a shimmering blue patch may appear on the ground. Many thirsty desert travelers have mistaken such mirages for pools of water. The same "pools" sometimes appear on highways on hot days.

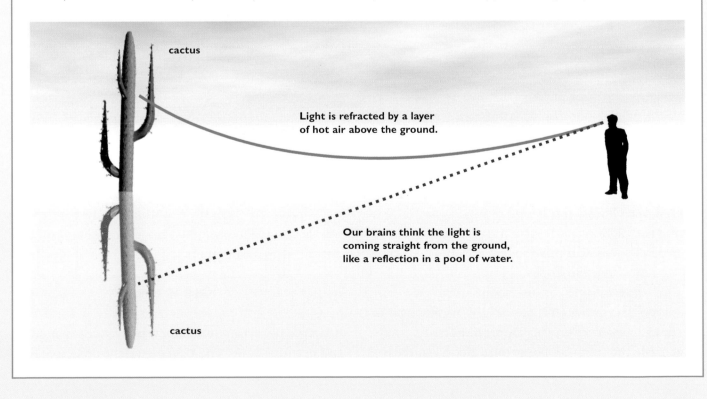

cactus

Light is refracted by a layer of hot air above the ground.

Our brains think the light is coming straight from the ground, like a reflection in a pool of water.

cactus

ACTIVITY 5
TELESCOPE

We can't pull down the Moon to have a better look at it, so we have to reach out to it with a telescope. Most telescopes use light to give us clearer pictures of faraway objects. Some use other forms of energy, such as radio waves.

To look at distant objects that human eyes cannot normally see, people use telescopes. The word telescope means "distance viewer." A telescope focuses light into an image that someone can then see through a strong magnifying lens. Astronomers use the world's largest telescopes to look at stars. In the past, ships' captains used handheld telescopes to see land or other ships in the distance. Today, we often use similar telescopes at scenic view spots.

There are two types of telescope. The type used by ships' captains of old and those found at tourist attractions are refracting telescopes. The largest astronomical telescopes are another type, called reflecting telescopes.

The oldest type of telescope, the refracting telescope, has lenses that bend light and focus it toward the observer's eye. Though nobody knows who made the first telescope, most people agree that the first person to sell them was Hans Lippershey

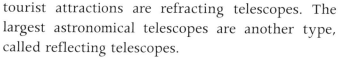 *Larger telescopes can see objects farther away. Amateur astronomers use small telescopes like this one to look at planets.*

(1570–1619), a Dutch eyeglass maker. In 1608 he used eyeglass lenses to make a simple telescope. The next year Galileo Galilei (1564–1642), an Italian scientist and astronomer, built his own telescope and became the first person to use a telescope to study the Moon and the planets. About 60 years later the English scientist Isaac Newton (1642–1727) invented the reflecting telescope. It had mirrors that focused light and was better for looking at very dim objects, such as distant stars and planets.

REFRACTOR

A simple refracting telescope has two lenses at either end of a long tube. The larger lens (the objective lens) is positioned at the front end. Light comes in through

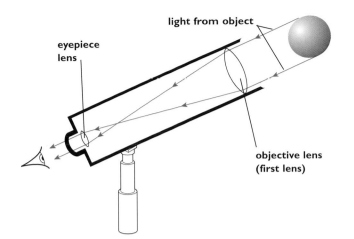

A refracting telescope uses the first lens to focus light onto the second lens, which magnifies the image.

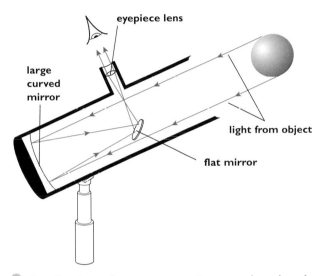

A reflecting telescope uses mirrors rather than lenses to focus light onto the eyepiece lens.

the objective lens and is focused to a point in front of the second lens, called the eyepiece. The image formed by the objective lens is magnified by the eyepiece lens so the observer can see the details.

The image appears larger and brighter, but upside down. That does not matter with stars, because there is no up or down in space. However, refracting telescopes used to look at objects on Earth need a certain arrangement of lenses or a combination of lenses and mirrors to turn the image the right way up.

REFLECTOR

Many reflecting telescopes look very different from refracting telescopes because they do not have a tube joining the parts together. To see very dim objects, telescopes need to collect a lot of light and must be very wide. Making wide lenses is expensive and difficult because the lenses are too heavy and bend under their own weight, producing distorted images. It is much easier to make large mirrors from light materials, and so the biggest telescopes are reflectors. They are used by astronomers and are usually built high up on mountains above the clouds. Instead of an objective lens, reflectors have a large curved mirror at the back of the telescope that reflects light forward onto another smaller mirror in front. This smaller mirror is angled so that it reflects the light into the eyepiece lens to be magnified for the observer's eye.

Hubble vision

The Hubble Space Telescope is a huge reflecting telescope that orbits the Earth to get the best possible view of objects in deep space, such as the farthest galaxies. Its 8-foot (2.4m) mirror was found to be faulty after the telescope was put in orbit, but astronauts fixed it by adding extra mirrors. Hubble was put into space to avoid the distortions caused by Earth's atmosphere.

The central tubular section (right) contains the mirror and other optical instruments. The two golden wings are solar panels. They use energy from the Sun to power the telescope.

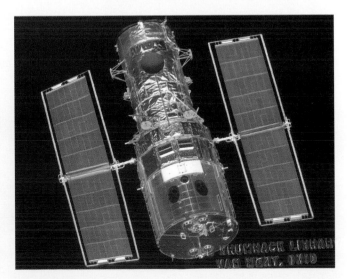

Make a Telescope

Goals

1. **Make a refracting telescope.**
2. **Find a distant object and see it in focus.**

What you will need:

- selection of glass or plastic lenses
- 2 cardboard tubes (one slightly narrower than the other, so it fits snugly inside the larger one)
- tape

1 Choose two lenses that will work together. To do this, hold one lens near your eye and a larger lens farther away. Look through them at a distant object, then move the larger lens until the object is in focus. Your cardboard tubes will need to be as long as the distance between the lenses.

2 Rest the larger lens on one end of the larger cardboard tube. Put a strip of tape around the end of the tube, and then press it down gently to hold the lens in place.

Troubleshooting

My telescope doesn't hold its focus very well.
Make sure that you get tubes that fit together snugly. If they don't, the lenses won't stay lined up when you slide the tubes in and out. The other thing that helps you focus is a steady hand. If you need to, rest the end of the telescope on a piece of furniture or a window ledge.

3 Place the small lens on the end of the small tube, and tape it in place.

Binoculars

Binoculars are like two telescopes stuck together, so each eye has a telescope. Binoculars are better for judging distances than telescopes because the brain needs images from both eyes to work out distances accurately.

Safety tip

Never use a telescope to look directly at the Sun. The focused light could damage your eyes forever and may even blind you. Likewise, avoid looking at lights through a telescope.

4 Slide the open end of the small tube into the large one. Choose an object at a distance, and try to bring it into focus by moving the small tube in and out of the large tube.

FOLLOW-UP Make a telescope

You can make a reflecting telescope using a shaving mirror (or another large, curved mirror), a small flat mirror, and a magnifying glass. It is important that the larger mirror you use is curved because the curve focuses light from the object you want to look at onto the smaller mirror. The Moon is a good choice of distant object to view. Remember never to look at the Sun or other bright objects with any telescope or binoculars.

Place the shaving mirror in front of the object you wish to view. Hold or place the flat mirror in front of the shaving mirror so that you can see the image reflected off the larger mirror in the smaller one. Then position the magnifying glass over the small mirror so that you can see a larger image of the Moon, or the object you have chosen to look at.

If you cannot see much detail, it may be because there is too much light coming from other sources. That is why telescope lenses and mirrors are placed inside tubes—the tubes cut out unwanted light. It is most fun to use this telescope at night to look at the Moon and stars.

ANALYSIS
Telescope

Refracting and reflecting telescopes use the light given off by an object to create an image of it. So, they are called optical telescopes. For hundreds of years optical telescopes were the only kind available.

However, visible light is just one type of electromagnetic radiation that comes from the Sun and stars. Heat, x-rays, radio waves, and ultraviolet radiation are among the other types produced. In the 20th century telescopes were built to detect these forms of electromagnetic radiation as well. Some of these unusual telescopes are built in a way similar to optical telescopes, using mirrors and lenses. The pattern of electromagnetic radiation that the telescope detects from the object in space is fed into a computer to create colored images that human eyes can see.

By contrast, radio telescopes do not have mirrors or lenses. Instead, they collect radio waves using large antennas. The first radio telescope was a collection of long wires on posts, and it looked a bit like an enormous washing line. Modern radio telescopes are giant dishes that can be pointed at different parts of the sky. A computer then maps where the waves came from and turns the information into a picture of the sky.

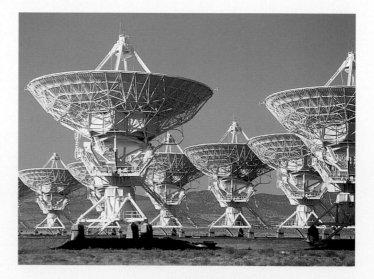

Radio telescope dishes focus radio waves onto a small detector, which then sends the signal to a computer to be turned into a picture.

ACTIVITY 6
TOTAL INTERNAL REFLECTION

When you make a phone call, your voice is turned into thousands of pulses of light that travel along fiber-optic cables. The cables trap the light inside thanks to a phenomenon termed total internal reflection.

See-through materials like glass and water usually let light pass right through, but sometimes light can get trapped inside. If a ray of light within the material hits the surface at a sufficiently shallow angle, it bounces back inside. When this effect, called total internal reflection, happens in raindrops, it makes a rainbow. It also makes diamonds so sparkly. Thanks to total internal reflection, fiber-optic cables can carry light around corners and across great distances without leaking. These cables contain hundreds of thin glass fibers, each of which carries pulses of light.

Total internal reflection occurs when light tries to pass into something with a lower refractive index (see page 23) than its current medium, for example, from glass into air. Reflection occurs when the angle of incidence—the angle at which the light strikes the boundary—is above a

Fiber-optic cables are bundles of thin glass fibers, each of which can trap pulses of light inside. The pulses of light carry information, TV pictures, or phone calls in a digital code.

certain amount, called the critical angle. Remember, the angles of light rays are measured from an imaginary line called the normal, which is at right angles—90 degrees—to the boundary (see page 11).

If the angle of incidence is more than the critical angle, the light reflects off the boundary instead of passing through. If the angle of incidence is less than the critical angle, the light passes out but is refracted (bent) away from the normal. If a light beam hits the boundary at exactly the critical angle, something interesting happens. The light is refracted to an angle of 90 degrees from the normal. In other words, the refracted light ray travels along the boundary between the two media.

In this activity you'll find out what happens when a beam of light from a flashlight gets trapped inside water by total internal reflection.

ACTIVITY

Trapped Beam

Goals

1. **Trap a light beam in a tank of water.**
2. **Measure the critical angle for water.**

What you will need:

- *glass tank full of water*
- *milk*
- *bright flashlight with a narrow beam or a projector beam at a narrow setting*
- *washable felt-tip pen*
- *protractor*
- *assistant*
- *ruler*

1 Clean the tank thoroughly, and fill it with the water. Add a tiny bit of milk. You should still be able to see through the water clearly. Close the curtains, and turn out the lights.

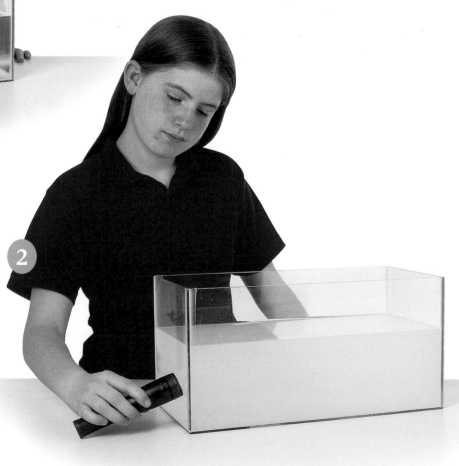

2 Shine the light through the side of the tank. Angle the beam upward so that it hits the water surface from below. Is the light reflected back down, or does it emerge into the air? Or do both happen?

3 Move the flashlight so that the beam hits the surface at different angles. Can you find the critical angle? That is when the light travels along the surface.

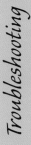

Troubleshooting

What if I can't see the beam?
Use less milk. You only need a few drops of milk to make the beam show up clearly.

What if the beam splits at the water surface?
Unless you use a laser, the beam will split at the surface. Try to find the angle where the light stops emerging into the air. It might help if you sprinkle some talcum powder in the air above the tank to make the emerging beam show up.

4 When you've found the critical angle, use the felt-tip pen to mark the beam's path with crosses on the front of the tank up to the water surface.

5 Draw through the crosses with a ruler to make a straight line. Where the line meets the water surface, draw a vertical line. This is the normal.

6 Use the protractor to measure the angle between the two lines. It is the critical angle for water.

FOLLOW-UP Trapped beam

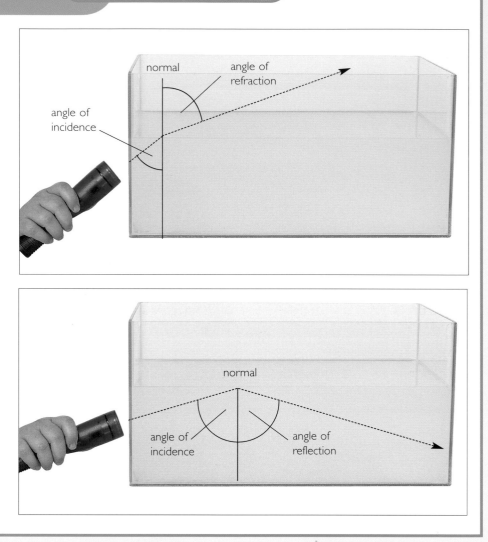

You can use your tank to investigate the relationship between the angles of incidence, reflection, and refraction.

Place the flashlight in different positions, and measure the angle of incidence each time in the same way as you measured the critical angle in the main activity. If the light is reflected back down, measure the angle of reflection (the angle between the normal and the reflected beam). If the light emerges into the air, measure the angle of refraction (between the normal and the emerging beam). If the refracted beam is difficult to see, use a piece of white paper to track it through the air.

Write down your results in a table, and see if you can find a pattern in the numbers.

ANALYSIS
Total internal reflection

In the main activity you should have measured the critical angle as being about 49°. It is difficult to measure accurately with a flashlight because the beam spreads out, but you could get a better result if you ask an adult to use a penlight laser instead. In the follow-up you would have found that the angle of incidence and angle of reflection are always equal, while the angle of refraction is always greater than the angle of incidence.

Total internal reflection happens because light speeds up when it moves from water into air or from glass into air. The increase in speed makes the emerging light ray bend away from the normal and back toward the water surface. If the light ray strikes the water surface from below at a shallow angle (a big angle from the normal), the change in direction sends it back under water. Instead of leaving the water slightly bent, it is reflected back down.

The water surface is actually better at reflecting light than a mirror, providing you look at it from the right angle. You can see this for yourself by looking up at the surface of the water from the side of the tank. If you keep fish in an aquarium, you've probably noticed that a very clear reflection is often visible under the surface. Unlike a mirror, which creates a slight double image due to reflection off the top and bottom of the glass, this water reflection is pin-sharp.

Glass has a higher refractive index than water and a lower critical angle. That means it can trap a light beam more easily. The glass fibers in a fiber-optic cable work like flexible light pipes. Light shining into one end travels through the glass and bounces off the walls of the fiber. Because it always hits the wall at an angle greater than the critical angle, it always reflects completely. The light travels unaffected all the way to the other end of the fiber, which may be thousands of miles away. TV and phone cables are made of many bundles of glass fibers. Surgeons also use fiber-optic cables to slide tiny cameras and lights into a person's body during so-called keyhole surgery.

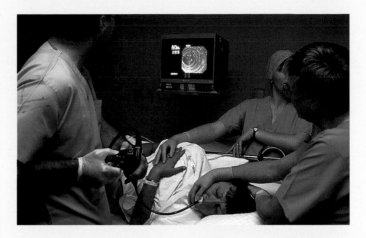

A camera at the end of a fiber-optic cable enables this surgeon to look inside his patient's lungs.

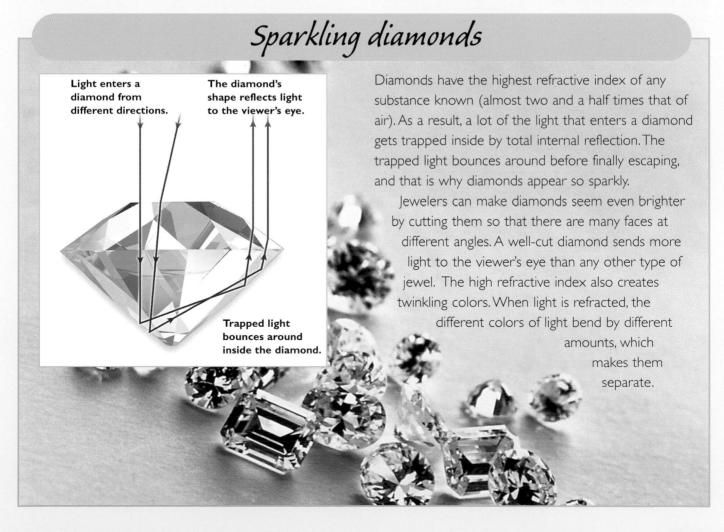

Sparkling diamonds

Light enters a diamond from different directions.

The diamond's shape reflects light to the viewer's eye.

Trapped light bounces around inside the diamond.

Diamonds have the highest refractive index of any substance known (almost two and a half times that of air). As a result, a lot of the light that enters a diamond gets trapped inside by total internal reflection. The trapped light bounces around before finally escaping, and that is why diamonds appear so sparkly.

Jewelers can make diamonds seem even brighter by cutting them so that there are many faces at different angles. A well-cut diamond sends more light to the viewer's eye than any other type of jewel. The high refractive index also creates twinkling colors. When light is refracted, the different colors of light bend by different amounts, which makes them separate.

ACTIVITY 7
PINHOLE CAMERA

Photographs are made when a certain amount of light is allowed onto a film at the back of a camera. The first cameras had a screen instead of a film and only a pinhole to let in the light. They were called camera obscuras.

Imagine you are sitting in a room with no windows at all. The door is closed; no light can get in from the outside. You sit with your back to one wall and see nothing. Now imagine that a hole is made in the wall behind you, above your head. The hole is tiny, a pinprick. Suddenly, a picture of the world outside the room appears on the wall in front of you. The room has become a camera obscura—a simple optical device that works in the

The world's first photo, taken with a pinhole camera by Joseph Niepce in 1822. The exposure time (when the light was allowed onto the film) was eight hours.

same way as a photographic camera, but which was invented hundreds of years earlier.

The words *camera* and *obscura* are Latin for "dark chamber." However, it was not the Romans who invented the camera obscura. The Greek philosopher Aristotle, who lived about 300 B.C., knew how to make and use a camera obscura. The great thinkers of the Islamic world also used the device, around 1,000 years ago, for studying the Sun.

The camera obscura began to be used again during a period of European history called the Renaissance (meaning "rebirth"). During the period, which lasted from the 14th to the 17th century, scholars in Italy rediscovered the knowledge of the ancient Greeks.

Renaissance artists used portable camera obscuras to help them paint landscapes and buildings accurately. The camera obscura was positioned in front of the scene so that an image appeared on a screen in the back of the device. The artist then traced this scene and painted in colors and other details. The Italian artist Canaletto (1697–1768) made many beautiful paintings of Venice this way.

FURTHER DEVELOPMENTS

In the 19th century this new optical technology was turned into tourist attractions and toys. Large camera obscuras were built for the public. The image, which was originally upside down, was flipped the right way around with an angled mirror that reflected it onto a domed roof, creating a circular image of the world outside.

The Victorians made smaller versions, too. They worked in exactly the same way as the original room-sized ones, but the image was viewed on a paper screen that made up the back wall of the device. Today we call these simple devices pinhole cameras.

Of course, many people wanted to record the images they saw with the camera and to keep them forever. By the 1830s two Frenchmen, Joseph Nicéphore Niepce (1765–1833) and Louis Jacques Mandé Daguerre (1787–1851), had both come up with ways of doing that using light-sensitive chemicals. They were coated onto sheets of metal or glass and held inside the camera. Niepce and Daguerre had invented photographs, but they were not like the ones we know today. It was not until about 100 years ago that flexible photographic film was developed, and the pinhole changed to a shutter.

Modern digital cameras use light-sensitive electronics to capture images. However, the way the light gets into the camera and forms an image is the same as in the basic darkened chamber of the camera obscura.

Dark sun

One important scientific use of camera obscuras was for observing solar eclipses. An eclipse happens when Earth, the Sun, and the Moon all line up, and the one in the center prevents the light from the other two from reaching each other. A solar eclipse occurs when the Moon is between the Sun and Earth and blocks most of the sunlight from reaching Earth. As the disk of the Moon moves across the Sun, the amount of light reaching Earth falls until all that remains is a small halo of light that shines past the black disk of the Moon.

It is very difficult to watch a solar eclipse happen because, while the Moon is only partially covering the Sun, the sunlight is still blinding. Only for the few seconds that the Moon covers the whole Sun can the eclipse be safely observed. That is why ancient astronomers began to use

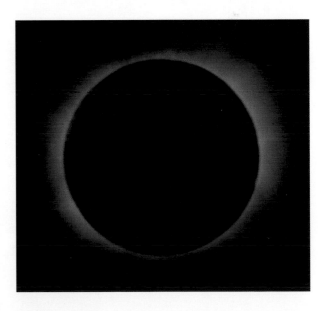

the camera obscura. They could safely look at the Sun and Moon during an eclipse as an image inside the camera obscura.

Make a Pinhole Camera

Goals

1. Make a pinhole camera.
2. Experiment with making images appear on a small screen.

What you will need:

- shoebox
- paintbrush
- black paint
- newspaper
- scissors
- tape
- tracing paper
- thick aluminum foil
- pin

1 Paint the inside of the box, including the lid, black.

Big and small

The size of camera obscuras varied. They could be models the size of a room that several people could fit into to view an eclipse of the Sun, or pocket-sized models that artists used to help them paint an outside scene.

2 Cut a small square out of either end of the box.

3 Cover one of the holes in the box with aluminum foil. Keep the foil tight, and tape down the edges so that no light can get in.

4 Cover the hole at the other end with tracing paper. Again, keep it taped tightly in place.

Troubleshooting

What if I can't see anything on the paper screen?

This camera will work better if you stand in a darkened room and look at objects outside. If you cannot see anything, you may have a light leak in your camera spoiling the image, or the inside of the box is not black enough, and light is bouncing around inside. The foil may also be too thin and be letting light through. In this case try a camera with a hole in the box itself.

5 Put the lid on the box. If the fit is not very tight, tape around the lid to hold it in place. Make sure you cover all the gaps.

6 Carefully make a hole in the center of the foil with a pin. Make the hole as tiny as possible. You have now made a pinhole camera.

7 Point the foil end of your pinhole camera at a suitable scene. Look at the image that is formed on the paper screen.

FOLLOW-UP · Make a pinhole camera

You can convert your bedroom, living room at home, or a classroom at school into a large camera obscura like the ones used in the 19th century.

Choose a room that has a window with a nice outside view. Cover all the windows in the room with black construction paper. Tape the paper down tightly. Make sure the room is completely sealed so that no light at all can get in. You may also need to tape around the door.

Get an adult's permission to move any furniture and paintings so that there is a blank wall opposite the window with a view, and nothing is blocking it.

Make a tiny pinhole in the paper covering the window with a view. Turn out all the lights in the room. An image of the view outside should appear on the wall opposite the window.

ANALYSIS
Pinhole camera

Camera obscuras are very simple. They work by letting in only a tiny amount of light. The rest of the light coming from a scene is blocked from entering the camera and is not seen by the observer.

Inside the camera the light appears to start at a single point. It has not been changed in any way and carries on until it hits the paper screen or wall, depending on the size of the device. The image that is formed by the light is upside down. That is not unusual; in fact, it happens just the same in our eyes, only our brains turn the image the right way up.

The reason the image is upside down is simple: light travels in straight lines. Think of a tree, for example. A ray of light that is traveling upward from the base of the tree toward the pinhole passes through it and carries on in the same direction, until it hits the back of the camera. It leaves a point of light at the top of the screen. Similarly, a ray of light from the top of the tree that is traveling down toward the pinhole travels through it in a straight line and illuminates the bottom of the screen. Light from all the points of the tree in between these two enters the camera in the same way and makes points of light in the correct place on the screen. Overall, an upside down image of the tree is formed.

HOLE SIZE

The hole in the front of a camera is called the aperture. When you made the aperture bigger, you should have seen the image get brighter but more fuzzy. The brightness is a result of letting more light in. The fuzziness comes from the image being produced by more than one point of light coming into the camera. This causes several separate images to form on the screen in slightly different positions, which, when combined, form a single blurred picture.

Although the image produced by a tiny point of light entering the camera is sharp, it is not easy to see because it is also very dim. That is because only a tiny amount of light can get through a tiny hole. So how do you get a sharp image as well as a bright one?

Before the invention of glass lenses, about 450 years ago, the camera obscura could only be used to view very bright objects, such as the outside world on sunny days and, of course, the Sun and the Moon. Lenses overcame this limitation. A lens can take in much more light than a tiny hole, yet the light is still focused to make a sharp image. As well as making the image brighter, lenses allow cameras to take photographs more quickly. In the early days of photography pinhole camera users had to leave their cameras still for minutes or even hours to collect enough light to make a picture. With a lens this time was cut down to mere seconds.

SHAPE AND DISTANCE

The lens in the human eye is much cleverer than those in cameras because it can change its shape and, therefore, its focal length. That allows the eye to focus images of objects at different distances. A glass lens has a fixed shape and always focuses an image at a certain point behind it. Instead of changing the shape of a camera lens, photographers alter the distance between the lens and the film to bring images at different distances into focus.

A wildlife photographer uses a long telescopic lens, which has a long focal length, to help her photograph animals a long way away without disturbing them.

If you widen the pinhole and put a lens in it, you will notice that you can only see sharp images of objects a particular distance away. Try making the camera with longer and shorter boxes so that you can focus on images at different distances from you. You could also try using different lenses.

How our eyes work

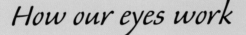

Our eyes work like miniature pinhole cameras. The pupil is the aperture, the size of which is controlled by the iris. The iris responds to the amount of light there is. Behind each pupil is a small lens that focuses light on the "screen" at the back of the eyeball. This "screen" is called the retina, and is made up of light-sensitive cells that convert the image formed into electrical signals that the brain turns into pictures. The picture on the retina is upside down, but the brain learns to turn it the right way up.

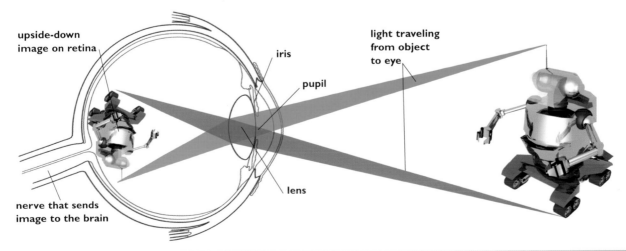

upside-down image on retina

iris

pupil

light traveling from object to eye

lens

nerve that sends image to the brain

ACTIVITY 8
DIFFRACTION

When light waves travel through tiny gaps, they spread out like ripples on a pond and interfere with each other. This interference can help scientists study light. We call the process diffraction.

Diffraction can make amazing patterns of colors. This one was produced by shining a strong white light through a set of tiny slits.

Have you ever wondered why you can hear around corners? It's thanks to something called diffraction. Sound is caused by waves in air; and like all waves, sound waves diffract. Diffraction simply means spreading out. When a sound wave passes the edge of an object or travels through a gap, it spreads out in all directions. Diffraction is most apparent when the wave travels through a gap narrower than the wavelength. In the case of sound this could be a doorway. As the wave emerges from the gap, it spreads out like a ripple on a pond, just as if it had been formed for the first time.

Light waves also diffract, but that is harder to show because light has a very short wavelength—many millions of times smaller than the wavelength of sound. As a result, light only diffracts when it passes through the tiniest of gaps.

If you've read the earlier activities, you'll know by now that white light is really a mixture of all the different colors. We can use diffraction to separate these colors and make a rainbow pattern called a spectrum. To do this, we use a device called a diffraction grating—a piece of glass etched with hundreds of microscopic slits.

Each slit in a diffraction grating makes the light passing through it diffract. The waves emerging from all the different slits are slightly out of phase, so they interfere with each other. Some wavelengths (colors) of light strengthen each other, while others cancel each other out.

The result of all this interference is a smooth spectrum of colors, which you can see if you look through a diffraction grating at a light. Diffraction gratings are very useful. The spectrums they produce are very clear and bright, which makes it easy

🔲 *This scientist can tell what chemicals are in the glass jars by using a spectrometer to analyze the light shining through them.*

to measure how much of each color is present. Diffraction gratings are used in machines called spectrometers that allow us to analyze light very carefully. When light from a particular source, such as a candle or a star, passes through a spectrometer, it produces a distinctive pattern like a fingerprint. By studying these patterns, scientists can identify the chemicals that produced the light or the chemicals that the light passed through on its way to the spectrometer.

The activity on the next page shows you how to build your own spectrometer with a shoe box and a homemade diffraction grating made from window screen. You can use it to study light from streetlamps, flashlights, screens, and other sources.

Thomas Young's discovery

One of the first people to study the diffraction of light was the English scientist Thomas Young (1773–1829). About 200 years ago Young shined a light through two pinpricks and found that it made a pattern of bright and dark bands on a screen. He concluded that light must travel in waves, since only waves can interfere with each other to make that kind of pattern. Young was correct, but other scientists pooh-poohed his theory. At the time, most people believed the rival theory, put forward by Isaac Newton (1642–1727), that light travels as a stream of particles. Because Newton was a much more famous and important scientist, few people took Young's results seriously. However, we now know that both men were right, and that light behaves as a wave and as particles at the same time.

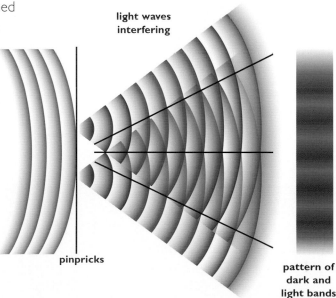

light waves interfering

pinpricks

pattern of dark and light bands

ACTIVITY

Make a Spectrometer

Goals

1. **Prove that light travels in waves.**
2. **Use a spectrometer to make a spectrum.**

- *shoebox*
- *scissors*
- *tape*
- *construction paper*
- *fine-mesh window screen*
- *lens*
- *flashlight*
- *colored pencils*
- *white paper*
- *modeling clay*

1 Cut a hole about 2 inches (5cm) square in each end of the shoebox. Tape two pieces of construction paper over one hole so that the pieces almost touch, leaving a vertical slit that lets a sliver of light into the box.

2 Cut three pieces of window screen to fit over the hole, and overlap them unevenly so the holes in each piece are partly blocked. Hold this screen "sandwich" over the hole, then look through it toward a light. Turn it around until you can see colors, then tape it in place.

Diffraction grating

You can use a commercial diffraction grating instead of window screen if you prefer. Ask an adult to get one for you. The stores in some hands-on science centers or science museums sell diffraction gratings. Your science teacher might also be able to lend you one.

3 Put the lid on the box—you now have a spectrometer! Shine a light into the slit, and hold the lens in front of the mesh. Place the white paper on the table—a spectrum should appear on it.

4 You can hold the lens in place with a blob of clay while you copy the spectrum onto the white paper with your colored pencils.

Troubleshooting

What if there's no spectrum?
If there's no spectrum, try turning the screen around by a quarter turn. It might also help to tape down the shoebox lid to keep light from leaking in. If there's still no spectrum, widen the slit a little, or use a brighter light. Closing the curtains and turning out the lights will help you see the spectrum.

FOLLOW-UP Make a spectrometer

Try making a spectrum from other sources of light, such as a colored light bulb, a streetlamp, or a computer screen set to a particular color. To analyze starlight, look through the window screen while holding the box toward a cluster of bright stars. Never look through the spectrometer at the Sun in this way—it will damage your eyes.

There are other ways you can learn about diffraction without using a spectrometer or a diffraction grating. You can also see the effect of diffraction with a pair of pencils and a flashlight. Use the kind of flashlight that unscrews to reveal a bare bulb. Stand the flashlight on a table with the top screwed off. Tie the two pencils together with string or a rubber band, but put a small piece of tape or cardboard between the pencils to make a thin slit between them.

Hold the pencils in front of the flashlight, and look through the slit. You'll see a line of light at right angles to the slit. Squeeze the pencils together, and the light will fade. Just before it disappears, you should see bright and dark blobs appear on the line close to the flashlight bulb. These patterns are caused by light diffracting as it passes through the slit. The dark bands will have red and blue fringes caused by separation of the white light into colors.

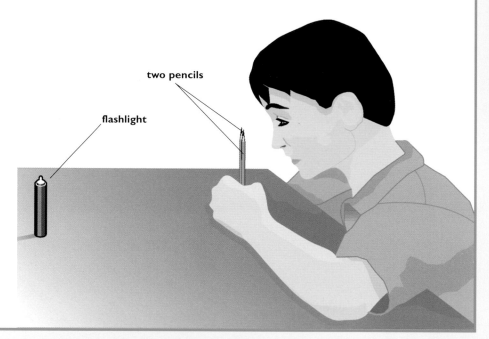

two pencils

flashlight

ANALYSIS
Diffraction

What can we learn from the colored spectrums produced by the spectrometer? Would you believe that astronomers can identify the atoms in stars billions of light-years away by using spectrometers? Not only that, they can tell how fast a star is moving from the color of light it produces.

Light is produced by atoms—the incredibly tiny particles that make up all types of matter. To understand how atoms produce light, you need to understand a little about the structure of atoms. Every atom has a center (a nucleus) and an outside. The outside is mostly empty, but it also contains tiny particles called electrons that whizz around the nucleus. When light hits an atom, the electrons become "excited"—they absorb energy from the light and move farther away from the atom's nucleus. Then they fall back to their original position and release the energy as light.

The color of light released by an atom depends on how far back the electron falls. If it falls a long way, the atom releases high-energy light. This has a short wavelength, which means it is near the blue end of the spectrum. If the electron falls a short way, the atom releases low-energy light, which has a long wavelength and is near the red end of the spectrum. Because different types of atoms have a different arrangement of electrons, they each

○ *Scientists can tell how fast galaxies and stars are moving through space by studying their spectrums.*

produce their own, characteristic range of colors when they release light. Sodium atoms, for instance, release yellow light. You can see this for yourself. Use your spectrometer to make a spectrum from a sodium streetlight (a yellow or orange streetlight). Instead of producing a whole spectrum of colors, the spectrometer will produce just a thin yellow line.

Different types of atoms also absorb characteristic colors. When astronomers study starlight with a spectrometer, they find black lines at places in the spectrum where they would expect to see color. The black lines are caused by atoms in the atmosphere of the star absorbing light of particular colors and so blocking it from reaching Earth. The position of the black lines tells astronomers exactly what types of atoms are in the star.

Not only does the light from stars tell us what kind of atoms they contain, but it can also tell us where a star is going. Light waves from a star get stretched or squeezed if the star is moving quickly, just as can sound waves from a motorcycle. When a motorcycle whooshes past, the noise it makes drops in pitch. That is because the sound waves are squashed together as it approaches, then stretched apart as it goes away. Sound waves with a short wavelength sound high pitched, while those with a long wavelength sound lower. Starlight shows a similar effect, but it varies in color rather than pitch. Astronomers call this effect red shift.

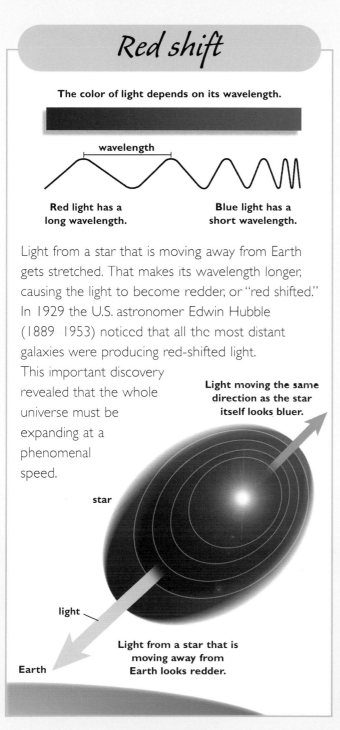

Red shift

The color of light depends on its wavelength.

wavelength

Red light has a long wavelength. **Blue light has a short wavelength.**

Light from a star that is moving away from Earth gets stretched. That makes its wavelength longer, causing the light to become redder, or "red shifted." In 1929 the U.S. astronomer Edwin Hubble (1889 1953) noticed that all the most distant galaxies were producing red-shifted light.

This important discovery revealed that the whole universe must be expanding at a phenomenal speed.

Light moving the same direction as the star itself looks bluer.

star

light

Earth

Light from a star that is moving away from Earth looks redder.

ACTIVITY 9
MOIRÉ PATTERNS

When patterns of repeating lines or dots are made to overlap, swirling bright and dark bands appear among them as if by magic. These fast-moving effects are called moiré patterns.

W hen a beam of light shines through a very narrow slit, the emerging light spreads out in waves (diffracts). If there are two slits close together, the light waves spreading out from each slit interfere with each other, producing a pattern of bright and dark bands on a screen.

Although we can see this pattern of bright and dark interference bands, it's hard to picture what's going on in the light waves. One way to understand light interference is to imagine ripples on a pond

A computer produced this multicolored moiré pattern. The circles interfere with the grid of dots (pixels) on the screen, producing more sets of circles.

crashing together and interfering. Another way is to use moiré (pronounced MWA-RAY) patterns.

Moiré patterns appear when you look through two overlapping patterns of lines, circles, or dots. A series of curving black bands suddenly appears and swirls or flows if the overlapping patterns move.

Shimmering silk

The word moiré comes from a type of fabric called mohair. In the 15th century, clothesmakers developed a technique to create shimmering, watery patterns on mohair, a bit like the moiré patterns seen in overlapping lines (but not formed by interference). Metal rollers pressed a ribbed pattern, or watermark, into the fabric. The pattern reflected light differently from the rest of the garment, creating a shimmering effect like water. Today clothesmakers use silk instead of mohair to create moiré effects. Moiré silk (left) is also called watered silk because of its luxuriously shiny appearance.

The bands in moiré patterns are caused by interference between the two original patterns. Where the lines from the two patterns coincide, they create a pale area. Where the black lines don't coincide, they create a dark area. A moiré pattern formed by two sets of concentric circles (circles of different sizes inside each other) is similar to the pattern of light interference formed by two slits (see page 45). Light waves ripple out from the slits as concentric circles, and where the circles overlap, they create bright and dark bands just like the bright and dark bands in a moiré pattern.

HERE, THERE, AND EVERYWHERE

Once you know how to recognize moiré patterns, you might start seeing them in some surprising places. The ripples that sometimes cross your TV screen or computer monitor are moiré patterns, for instance. You can also see moiré patterns in overlapping mesh fences, in the railings on the side of the bridge, or in the folds of a net curtain.

In this activity you can create moiré patterns in several different ways: by sliding combs or window screens over each other and by making overlapping patterns of black lines. You'll need to use a photocopier to make patterns on transparent plastic film, so ask an adult to help you before you begin.

The swirling gray bands that appear in the folds of net curtains are moiré patterns.

Making Moiré Patterns

Goals

1. **Make your own swirling moiré patterns.**
2. **Compare moiré patterns made by straight lines to patterns made by circles.**

What you will need:

- *two small combs*
- *thin pen*
- *paper*
- *ruler*
- *access to photocopier and transparencies*
- *thin mesh, such as a window screen*

1 Hold the combs in front of a light source (but not the Sun). Slowly move one in front of the other. Can you see patterns of lines that are not the combs' teeth?

Show me the money

Look closely at a banknote and you might see patterns of concentric circles printed in the paper. They make it difficult for criminals to forge the bills. When a bill with a fine pattern is copied on a color photocopier, a moiré pattern appears on the copy, making it useless.

2 Draw a pattern of close black lines or concentric circles (see page 54) on a piece of white paper. Photocopy this pattern onto two transparencies, and overlap them to make moiré patterns.

see page 54

Troubleshooting

How do I draw concentric circles?
The easiest way to draw neat concentric circles is to use a drawing program on a computer. Draw one large circle, copy and paste it over the first, then reduce its size a bit. Continue until you've filled the space in the first circle. If you don't have access to a computer or a photocopier, use compasses and a pen to draw the circles on tracing paper.

3 Slide two pieces of window screen over each other, and watch moiré patterns appear within them.

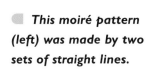

This moiré pattern (left) was made by two sets of straight lines.

FOLLOW-UP

Making moiré patterns

If you find it difficult drawing neat patterns of concentric circles or parallel lines, use the patterns below. Photocopy them onto transparencies, then overlap them in different combinations to see what kind of moiré patterns they make.

There are other ways you can create moiré patterns. If you have only one comb, for instance, hold a mirror behind it, and try to make a pattern by looking through the comb's teeth at the reflection.

Use a similar trick to make moiré patterns with a window screen. Place a piece of white paper behind a window screen on a sunny day, and the screen will form moiré patterns with its shadow. You can also see moiré patterns in thin, gauzy fabrics. Fold the fabric in two, and hold it up to the light, then slowly slide the layers around to make the pattern move.

Overlapping concentric circles make radiating dark bands like those seen here.

concentric circles

parallel lines

Photocopy these two templates twice each onto transparent plastic films. Overlap different combinations, and see what patterns they make.

ANALYSIS
Moiré patterns

Moiré patterns are caused by interference. Unlike the interference patterns we saw in Activity 2 (see pages 12–16), which formed from interfering light waves, moiré patterns occur when patterns of line or dots overlap.

When the combs passed each other, their teeth moved from alignment to misalignment and back again. As soon as the combs became misaligned, a pattern appeared. At first the pattern consisted of dark lines packed together tightly, but these lines quickly spread out.

The patterns in the transparencies and the window screen formed in the same way. When you moved the overlapping sheets, you probably noticed that the bright and dark bands in the moiré pattern moved much more quickly than the sheets themselves. This tendency of moiré patterns to magnify small movements is very useful. Engineers use it to detect cracks or other imperfections in the wings of airplanes and other machines. If a crack can be

detected early enough, it can be fixed before it becomes dangerous. Using a special viewer, the engineer compares the shape of the real object with a template that matches the preferred shape. If a moiré pattern appears when the two shapes overlap, there must be a crack or dent that has changed the object's shape slightly.

Moiré patterns can also be a nuisance. When printers make books, like this one, they produce photographs by combining many tiny colored dots. Look at any photograph in this book with a magnifying glass, and you'll see it consists of dots of only four colors: black, yellow, magenta (pink), and cyan (pale blue). Each photograph, therefore, consists of four overlapping patterns of dots. To prevent moiré patterns from appearing among the dots, the printers turn the original photograph around to different angles for each color. This prevents similar patterns from overlapping when the colors are combined.

Flashing cards

Use moiré patterns to make these playing cards flash before your eyes. First photocopy the black grid onto a transparency. Then slide the transparency slowly over each card, making sure the lines in the grid are perfectly vertical. The colored symbol on each card will expand and shrink as the grid passes over, making it appear to flash.

ACTIVITY 10
BLUE SKY

What makes the sky blue, sunsets red, and clouds white?
The answer lies in a process called scattering, which you can study
with just a flashlight and a glass of milky water.

The sky's color depends on the way sunlight interacts with the atmosphere—the layer of air trapped around Earth by gravity.

As everyone knows, sunlight is white. Catch sunlight on a piece of paper, and the brilliant light will dazzle you. Sunlight also looks white when it streams through dusty air, though the air itself is invisible. But if air is invisible and sunlight is white, why is the sky blue? And why does light seem to come from the whole sky, not just the Sun?

THE SKY'S THE LIMIT

In fact, air is not completely invisible. Air is a gas, and the molecules (tiny particles) in gases are spread out much more thinly than in solids or liquids. Most of the light striking a gas passes straight through, but a small amount of light gets scattered—it changes direction when it hits the gas molecules. Between the surface of Earth and outer space there are about a hundred miles of air. With all that gas in the sky, the light scattered by the air molecules adds up until we see it as the blue sky.

The different colors that make up white light get scattered by different amounts in air. The shorter the wavelength of light, the more easily it gets scattered. Blue has a short wavelength, so it is scattered very easily. Red and yellow light have longer wavelengths. They are not easily scattered, so they travel in a staight line to the ground as direct sunshine. When you look away from the Sun but into

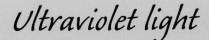

the sky on a clear day, you mostly see scattered light, and that is why the sky is blue. You might wonder why the sky isn't violet, since violet light has the shortest wavelength and is therefore scattered most easily. The answer is that sunlight contains more blue light than violet, and in any case our eyes see a mixture of blue and violet as blue.

The first scientists to discover why the sky is blue were the English physicists John Tyndall (1820–1893) and Lord Rayleigh (1842–1919). Tyndall and Rayleigh both thought the blue part of sunlight was scattered by dust and water vapor, but they were wrong. If dust was responsible, the sky would change color much more when the air is hazy. We now know that air molecules themselves are responsible for scattering light. Nevertheless, we still call this type of scattering the Tyndall effect, or Rayleigh scattering, after the two scientists.

The Tyndall effect works only when the particles doing the scattering are very small compared to the wavelength of light. Larger particles, such as cloud or fog droplets, scatter all wavelengths of light, not just blue. This type of scattering, called Mie scattering, explains why clouds are white. However, the biggest storm clouds can grow so tall that they let very little light through, which makes them look gray or even black from below.

Ultraviolet light

The shortest wavelength of light we can see is violet. Sunlight also contains a type of radiation known as ultraviolet (UV) light, which has a slightly shorter wavelength than violet but is invisible to human eyes. Although we can't see UV light, many insects can. Some flowers reflect UV light in stripes, producing colored patterns that only insects can see (below). UV light causes sunburn if we stay in the sun for too long, but our skin turns darker to protect us. Like blue and violet light, UV light is scattered easily by the air. As a result, you can get a suntan on a sunny day even when you're sitting in the shade.

Why are sunsets red?

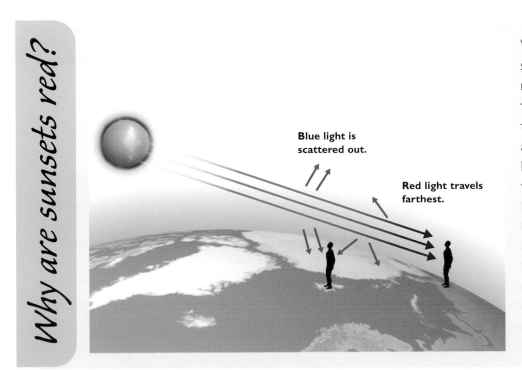

Blue light is scattered out.

Red light travels farthest.

When the Sun sets, the sky slowly turns orange and then red. That happens because the light has to travel through more and more air as the Sun gets nearer the horizon. With so much air to travel through, all the blue light gets scattered away. Red, orange, and yellow are left behind, which is why the Sun changes color. These colors also get scattered by dust in the air, producing spectacular colored patterns in the darkening sky.

ACTIVITY

Sunset in a Glass

Goals

1. Scatter light through a glass of milky water.
2. Find out which colors are scattered most easily.

What you will need:

- large glass or vase
- water
- milk
- powerful flashlight
- colored plastic sheets

1 Fill the glass with water, and add a small amount of milk.

Volcanic sunsets

The best sunsets happen after a huge volcano erupts. Ash from the volcano rises high into the atmosphere and blows around the planet. The tiny ash particles scatter red light, making the sky around the Sun much redder than usual.

2 Shine the flashlight through one side of the glass. Look at the beam from the opposite side, from the same side as the flashlight, then from halfway between.

3 Shine the flashlight through a colored plastic sheet, and look at the glass from all around again. Does the beam look any different?

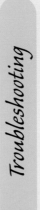

Troubleshooting

What if I can't see the beam?
Your flashlight might not be powerful enough. If you are using the most powerful one you have, try putting in new batteries. Also, make sure there isn't too much milk in the water, which would block the beam completely. It will also help if you turn out the lights and close the drapes.

Red sky at night

Sometimes the sky turns red just before the Sun rises, or just after the Sun sets. That is caused by Earth's atmosphere refracting (bending) sunlight from below the horizon.

4 Try using different colored sheets if you have them. Write down your results for each color.

FOLLOW-UP **Sunset in a glass**

The activity works better if you use an aquarium instead of a glass. If your flashlight is powerful enough, you should be able to see the color of the beam change along its length.

You can produce a much brighter beam by using a slide projector. Ask an adult to help you set up the projector as follows. First, cut out a square of black cardboard or plastic to fit inside in a slide mount. Make a hole in the square with a punch, then set the square in the mount. Place the slide in the projector, and focus the lens to produce a sharp beam.

You can change the beam's appearance by looking through a polarizing filter from a camera. Polarizing filters are designed to darken the blue sky so that

clouds stand out in photographs. Look through the filter at the tank, and slowly turn the filter around in your hand. What happens to the beam?

ANALYSIS
Blue sky

The milky water scattered light in the same way as the atmosphere does. When you looked at the water from the same side as the flashlight, it should have looked slightly bluish around the beam. From the far side it should have looked slightly red. Blue light is scattered most easily, which is why the water near the flashlight turned blue. In contrast, red light penetrates farthest, making the water at the far side redder. Light viewed from the side of the glass should have looked white because it contained equal amounts of all the colors.

The colored sheets converted the light beam into one color. The milk scattered the light as before, but the color should have looked the same from any direction.

If you used the polarizing filter in the follow-up, you would have discovered that the beam brightened and faded as you rotated the filter. That happens because of an effect called polarization. As you might know, light travels as a wave, a bit like ripples on the surface of a pond. However, while water waves only wobble up and down, light waves wobble at all angles. When white light is scattered, it becomes polarized—all the waves scattered in a particular direction are wobbling at the same angle. The polarizing filter blocks out such polarized light. As the filter turns, it blocks different angles of polarized light, making the beam turn bright and dark. You can see a similar effect by looking through the filter at a blue sky.

▶ *Blue morphos are among the largest and most beautiful butterflies in the world. Their stunning colors come from scattered light, not from a blue pigment.*

The first person to carry out the milky water experiment was the English physicist John Tyndall. The blue color that the Tyndall effect produces is not just seen in the sky. The beautiful blue morpho butterflies of South and Central America, for instance, get their shiny blue color from the Tyndall effect. The wing scales of blue morphos are covered by microscopic blobs that are small enough to scatter blue light but allow other colors past. The other colors are absorbed by a layer of black pigment below the blobs. Many green lizards and frogs get their color in a similar way, but the scattered blue light turns green when it passes through an overlying layer of yellow pigment. If the yellow layer is removed from the skin of these animals, they turn blue.

The Tyndall effect also causes the blue haze that sometimes hangs over mountain forests. In this case the blue light is scattered not by air molecules but by chemicals called terpenes, which escape from plants. The terpenes react with ozone (a form of oxygen) to form tiny particles that scatter blue light.

When the first pictures taken on Mars were sent back to Earth, scientists were very surprised to see that the sky was red. They had expected it to be a darker blue than Earth's, because Martian air contains a lot of carbon dioxide, which scatters blue light strongly. The scientists soon discovered that the sky was red because of rust-colored dust blown into the air by the fierce winds.

◀ *The sky on Mars is usually red because of windblown dust, but it turns dark blue in calm weather.*

GLOSSARY

amplitude: The height of a wave's crest.

angle of incidence: The angle of an incoming beam of light at any boundary.

angle of reflection: The angle of a reflected beam of light at a set boundary.

atmosphere: The envelope of gas that surrounds a planet. Earth's atmosphere is known as the air.

atom: The basic unit of an element. In an element all atoms share the same number of subatomic particles called protons and electrons.

camera obscura: An early form of pinhole camera that was a darkened room.

concave lens: A lens that is thinner in the middle and makes objects look smaller.

convex lens: A rounded lens. A convex lens makes objects look bigger.

crest: The top of a wave.

critical angle: The angle above which refraction occurs. Below the critical angle light is reflected back inside the substance.

diffraction: Spreading out in waves.

diffraction grating: A material cut through with hundreds of tiny slits.

diffuse light: Light that is reflected off a surface that is not mirrorlike.

electromagnetic radiation: Energy in wave form, including light, radio waves, x-rays, infrared, ulraviolet, and other waves.

electrons: Tiny charged particles that orbit the nucleus (center) of an atom.

excited: The state of electrons when atoms are hit by light or heat. The electrons move away from the nucleus, then move back to their original position, releasing the energy as light.

eyepiece: The lens in front of which light is focused in a refracting telescope.

focal length: The distance from a lens where light rays come together (converge) and form an image.

focus: Where light rays meet and form an image after traveling through a lens.

frequency: The number of wavelengths that pass a particular point in a second.

high-energy light: Light with a short wavelength near the spectrum's blue end.

index of refraction (refractive index): A number that compares the speed of light as it passes through a particular medium with the speed of light as it passes through space.

in phase (waves): Waves that reach their crest and trough at the same time.

interference: When waves combine and alter their original properties.

iris: Colored part of the eye.

medium: Any substance through which light passes.

microscope: A device that combines several lenses to magnify minute objects thousands of times to make them visible.

Mie scattering: The scattering of all wavelengths of light by larger particles.

mirage: A vision seen in the desert, and sometimes on the hot surface of a highway, caused by refraction of light.

mirror image: An image that is flipped from left to right or up to down.

moiré pattern: Swirling bands that seem to appear behind overlapping, repeating sets of lines and dots. This impression is caused by interference between the two different sets of patterns.

normal: An imaginary line that is at 90 degrees to a reflecting surface.

objective lens: Front lens in a refracting telescope.

optical telescope: A telescope that uses light given off or reflected by an object to create an image of it. Refracting and reflecting telescopes are both types of optical telescopes.

ozone: A naturally occurring colorless gas.

prism: A transparent, usually glass, shape used to separate light into colors.

pupil: The opening at the front of the eye through which light enters.

radio telescope: A telescope that focuses radio waves rather than light waves.

The waves are turned into a picture by a computer.

Rayleigh scattering: Another name for the scattering of light by air molecules.

red shift: The stretching (the shift toward longer wavelengths) of light from distant objects, such as stars, as they travel at speed away from Earth.

reflecting telescope: A telescope that is built with mirrors rather than lenses to focus light. Large astronomical telescopes are reflecting telescopes.

reflection: Light "bounced" back off the surface of water, glass, metal, and so on.

refracting telescope: A telescope in which lenses bend light and focus it toward the observer.

refraction: Light changing direction as it passes through water, glass, air, and the like.

Renaissance: The period of European history from the 14th to the 17th century, when scholars in Italy rediscovered the learning of ancient Greece and Rome.

retina: The light-sensitive cells that line the back of the inside of the eye.

scattering: Changes of direction of light as it hits gas molecules in the air. Because blue light scatters easily, the sky appears blue.

spectrometer: A machine that analyzes light. It measures wavelengths and angles of refraction and reflection.

spectrum: Band of colors— red, orange, yellow, green, blue, indigo, violet— produced when light shines through a prism.

telescope: A device that uses many lenses to magnify images of distant objects.

terpenes: Chemicals, released by plants, that react with ozone to form particles that can scatter blue light.

total internal reflection: Light trapped inside a material by bouncing back inside it. It occurs when light is at the wrong angle to escape into the other, less dense material.

transparent: See-through.

trough: The lowest part of a wave.

vacuum: A place that contains no matter at all.

wavelength: Distance between the crests of a wave.

SET INDEX